LOOKING at LIFE from an ANGLE

LOOKING at LIFE from an ANGLE

albert klassen

LOOKING at LIFE from an ANGLE

ISBN 978-1-7782809-0-0

All rights reserved. Except as permitted under (U.S. Copyright Act of 1976), or (Canadian Copyright Act of 2012), no part of this publication may be reproduced, distributed, or transmitted in any form or by any means, or stored in a database or retrieval system, without the prior written permission of the publisher.

Albert Klassen
albertklassen@icloud.com

Books by Albert Klassen

the death of the girl with the beautiful hair
looking at life from an angle
the life of lido pepperman
the church
radical madness
a monk in paradise
the abstract god
journey
never been to berlin

chapter one

a strange life
everyone's life is absurd when looked at from an
angle
how can this be or
whatever were you thinking or
is the air clean and pure up there or
when do you think is the end of time or
does time exist at all or
nothing

empty bubbles of nothing
how would we identify with that
how would we describe that
how would we explain that
those are questions people ask

and why do they even ask
is it like curiosity
the cat came back after it was satisfied
will Nancy ever come back
even if her favourite piece is played by an orchestra
at her favourite old church in Victoria
or maybe she prefers to be alone in her house with
her cats
Félix and Jones and Mozart

and all the kinfolk joined hands and danced around
the mulberry tree
singing songs of deliverance
giving thanks to angels and monks and gods
to be set free from the bondage that they were under

grotesque
what is strange
smoking a pipe in the attic
dangerous moves
moviemaking in a cellar with strangers
eating sardines and saltines

beaurocrats are heartless rats
who are they really
they're so weird
they rubber-stamp everything and act like mindless
robots
it annoys me
I don't know what to make of them

they're not really people at all
subhumans

rows and rows of guns lined up on shelves
ready for shooting and killing
I don't know why
but I don't want to die
they say that guns are good for defence
a good defence wins championships

amidst the chaos it feels strange
images of the war in Vietnam flash on the screen in
the corner

lost souls live in asylums
where white-clad people serve them
they have to keep them locked up
to protect them
it used to be hip to be nuts
but things have changed
now the lost souls live on the streets
and the politicians are smug about it
throwing their hands in the air
whatever

willy paddled out to sea
he wanted to feel free
he ate a fruit cup everyday
what can we say
he wanted to be a healthy guy

he didn't want to die

wipe that smirk off your face hoodlum
and straighten up your back
act like a proper human being and don't be so rude
are you an animal

barbecue on the beach
drunk all the time
music playing on the boom box
sleep in the tent
sleep all night
sleep till noon
eat a big steak for breakfast and keep drinking
smoke a joint
jump in the water and splash around
lay on a towel and drink in the sun
eat some chips and shrimp
and keep on drinking
then it's off to the tent to sleep
sleep all night
sleep till noon
wake up and eat a big juicy steak
and keep on drinking

chapter two

he met her at the bar and her name was Kate
she wasn't there to celebrate
but to drown her sorrow in a bottle of booze
and then go home and have a great big snooze
he took her home and tucked her into bed
she slept like she was dead
the next day he called her to see if she was okay
she said she was having a better day
in the evening they went out for a movie
it was groovy
now they're living together with a dog named Bob
and they like eating corn on the cob
such a nice story
to God be the glory

chapter three

men play with their wieners
women play with their pussys
what's wrong with that
what's wrong with that
it's taboo said the elders
do not pleasure yourselves unless
the wrath of God you wish to incur
and when you have sex
keep your clothes on
and ask one of the elders to supervise you so you
adhere to the rules
no no none of that
quickly in and then out and then off
and only missionary position
no doggy style

we're not animals
and no more kissing or dancing
keep your hands to yourself and focus on reading the
bible and prayer
keep from temptation
and women and men sleep in separate beds
sex is a necessary evil but it must be supervised by
the elders
thus says the lord of hosts
the lord god almighty
do not go against him and his precepts
be pure
be holy
be clean

cleanliness is next to godliness
and for heaven's sake smell good
wash with nice soap
and put on some nice perfume
and brush your teeth
and gargle with mouthwash
and change your undergarments every day
and shower once a day and have a bath once a day
and don't pee in the bath
use expensive shampoo even if you have to save and
scrimp
don't be a wimp
don't whine like a baby
head up
chin up

if you put it that way
you're asking me to trust and obey
but that's just not my way
I'd rather pay
my own way
you see I need to have a say
in how I live my own life okay

first they smile at you
then they buy you things
and before you know it they're living in your house
freeloading and eating all your food
and you say
hey
wait a minute
what happened here

vultures are all around
nasty people who use you and bully you
stay away from them
be your own person and do it your way
all those desperadoes who've got nothing better to
do than prey on you
bad bad backstabbers
cold hearted robbers
if they could
they would
steal your very soul
don't open the gate
wait

lock the door and turn on the music and dance alone
at least you will be safe

all those pastors and priests and rabbis
they want to tell you what to do
behind your back they're screwing your wife
silver tongued con men
religion is their tool
and with it they make a fool
of you
as they tell you that they speak to God
and God tells them secrets
and God puts them in charge of your life
so you obey them
please willy
don't be so silly
to give them the time of day
and don't let your woman worship them
as if they're rock stars
stay away from their cathedrals
stay away from their synagogues
stay away from their churches

dear lady I know that you are fine

oh the storms of life
people are dying
and some are crying
loneliness is hurting us
and the nights get so dark

and so long
we yearn and we pine
wishing they were still here
we sigh as we sip our beer

feel the ocean breezes
beside the ocean walking
blue water
the spray
it feels like eternity
with days lasting forever
holding the hand of your lover

will salvation ever come back
like a lonely lover
looking for a nesting place
somewhere to forgive all those sins committed
in moments of weakness
or despair
or in a fit of rage

chapter four

what if you were Italian instead of Swedish
how would that feel
they both make good meatballs
different but good

how is it that some people love to use big words
do they feel small within themselves
so they find big flowery and complicated words to
use
even though simple words will work just fine
are you a nerd
if you have to use a big word
to make yourself heard
above the rush of the traffic on Main Street
where everyone is lost

where everyone is trying to find their way
where everyone is trying to impress
see my dress how nice it is
what about my new Italian jeans
look at my new necklace and how it shimmers
I got a new haircut
can you tell
how about the new perfume I'm wearing
doesn't it smell nice
it goes good with my new shoes
oh I like your purse
where did you get it and what brand is it
love your glasses

Dick and Jane went to the restaurant
they ordered fish and chips
so good
yummy for the
tummy
then they paid the bill
and left a 15% tip
thank you
bye
the name of the waitress was Roxanne
she was working and going to university to become a teacher
she wanted to teach Highschool math
she was smart
she loved to eat bananas
she would eat like ten a day

she also liked coke
she drank a couple of cokes a day
she was blonde
she was pretty
she also liked to go to the beach and suntan
she was Swedish

chapter five

defeat is only for winners
those willing to dream
those willing to try
those with the courage to rise

chapter six

be careful with your smiles
why give them to everyone
save them for your lover
or your mother
and give them to your children especially
when they cry
or when they sigh

walking around like a moron
a big smile on their face
look at me I'm happy
and I'm snappy
I'm better than you because I smile all the time
no frown
just a smiling clown

strangers toasting each other over a pint

oh I love you
you are so cool
let me kiss your boots
no please kiss mine
my boots are from Brazil
mine are from Italy
oh I see

it's easy to fall in love
and then
what

noodles are falling from heaven
but where is the sauce

drifting through life like beatniks
casting our nets to this side
and then that
older and still wandering
like a gypsy
the wind blows and we don't know how to set our sails
please mad hatter tell me your secrets
so I can adjust my hat just right
the crowd of people at the monument tried to light the flare

the truth
the whole truth
and nothing but the untruth

the steps are small and feeble
and many times we fall
then who do we call

baby steps
into the chaos of anarchy
our shoes stuck in the mud
as the age of unreason begins
the nothing has come out of the cave
sweeping rhythmically with a corn broom
make it clean
what has been
is unclean
make it clean

the delinquents are spitting at the emperors feet
laughing in his face
so many freaks
what do they all want
unconstitutional actions are being taken by the high court
law and order is falling into a cauldron of evil
in the place where the witches of darkness cast spells
trying to drown out the good
and play soccer against the saints
without nets
without balls
without God

in the basement of the hotel lives an old man
keeping company with his memories
and painting endlessly
eating licorice and day old doughnuts brought to
him by Alice
he writes novels by candlelight
working deep into the night
a little bit of this and
a little bit of that
and when he's tired he sleeps in his king-sized four
poster bed
where sometimes Alice joins him

chapter seven

lifting high the standard
marching through the city gates
whereupon the jester doubled up in mirth
hi ho
the merry ho
oh Christmas tree thou are forever green
rich in things unseen
which natural eyes cannot but dream of
and about which sister Agnes has to pout
do it my way
it's the only way
my way or the highway
the foot stamping
still the soldiers march on as the people line the side
of the road

watching silently as the horror unfolded in front of them
their city taken over by a foreign army
and their peace shattered
futures insecure
lives changed forever

dam the changes
why can't things be left the same

rye bread
olives
liver sausage
rye and coke
a meal for the ages
created for jesters and sages

don't dance in the foyer of the Holiday Inn
it's here where newlyweds stay
to rest before the trials of life begin
as the end to innocence takes its toll
bringing them to their knees
and almost destroying their will to live
he wanted to stand so tall
but smashed his head on the wall
defeated he ran away
to hide and cry away from the fray
so God sent him an angel to help him again
and stop him from going insane

on the other side they chew their meat
counting sheep
and tearing apart old cars
salvaging all the parts and shipping them to Spain
to keep from going insane

be nimble little Jack
don't give your friend a wack
find a candlestick
and light the wick
be quick about it
and jump over it
reinvent yourself so we can see
another side
of yourself

in the courtroom Mr.Piddelty was accused of fraud
why did you forge the document sir
to gain some money your honour
didn't you know it was wrong
of course
do you take me for an imbecile
so you thought you'd get away with it
I was hoping
that was rather stupid
only if I got caught
which you did
would you do it again
if I could get away with it yes
what

I'm only being honest your honour
I'm not here to kiss your ass and suck up
so you have no regret
only that I got caught
well you are very honest Mr.Piddelty
I swore under an oath that I would tell the truth
the whole truth
and nothing but the truth
so I had to tell the truth
still I'm surprised because most come in here and lie
through their teeth
I'm an honest fella
not completely honest
that's true but
are any of us
that's true
okay then I give you two years in jail
thank you your honour
you're welcome sir

honesty is hard to find
with lies we protect ourselves
and there are many kinds of lies
some barefaced and others so subtle
we take shelter under shady trees
which hide the glare from the bright bright sun
that way we don't get sunburn
and stay comfortable

are you feeling good

how are you feeling
I hope you're feeling good
it's no fun to be sick and in pain
it will slowly drive you insane

take two asperins and don't call me in the morning

prescriptions for a good life can be found in the
pages of fashion magazines
wear this and don't put on that
use this lotion
it will take away your wrinkles
it will make you feel young again
that way you won't go insane

chapter eight

in a state of altered conscienceness we live
and what would we not give
to live in a mansion on a hill
taking a pill
feeling good all the time
never coming down and it's not a crime
psychedelic drugs conjure up sweet dreams
in the kitchen you will find some crispy cremes
it's so cool
you dive into your pool
naked ladies there to give you a massage
a Lamborghini in the garage
linen sheets on your bed
and your landscaper is a guy named Fred
or was it Ted

or maybe he's dead

she climbed the hill and looked back
the town looks so small from here
maybe I will drink a beer
and get drunk
smashed out of my tree
wouldn't that feel so free
dancing up and down the streets
exposing herself to anyone she meets
take a look at this
or this
or how about this

echoes of my interpretation of god's voice
ringing in my ear
why
leave me alone dear god
wanting to do my own thing
don't want to worry about doing your bidding
besides
your voice is in my imagination
it's made up
and our artists vision of who
you
are supposed to be
I can't be free
can't you see
everybody knows that we don't know God
and so

we try to be cool
but come off looking like a fool
because no matter where we stand
we don't understand

coincidently I used up the last piece of hope
put it in my porridge and it tastes so good
but now it feels like it's all over
and what am I to do
guess I'll walk over to the corner store
buy some Export A cigarettes
and smoke till midnight
pass the whiskey please
let's drink to our hopelessness
and cry in our drinks

mommy and daddy
Asherah and Yahweh
how many children did they have
were they all boys
Jesus was Asherah's stepson it seems
I bet it wasn't the first time Yahweh cheated on her
with an earthling
I wonder how mad she was
and what did she say to Jesus when he finally came home

perspective can be a dishonest merchant
selling us what we didn't know we bought
until we got caught

in a crossfire
and find we were a naive buyer
not checking out the goods
before we left the woods

just think how Isaak felt
after he being blind felt Jacob's arms and found them to be hairy
this is my firstborn said he and gave him the blessing meant for Esau

chapter eight-and-a-half

Jesus died to set us free
he was only thirty three
died for you and me
can't you see

chapter nine

living in a slum
being a bum
so much skum
are you glum
don't be dumb
where you from
walk down the street hohum
feeling so numb
go to the pub and drink some
rum
yum
and you sit in the corner and disappear
how small is your life
shrinking till you fade away
waiting for aunt dolly to buy you some shiny boots

of leather
that could lift your spirits and allow for a comeback

we love our French fries
cause they go so good with all the noble lies
we tell everyday
just a bunch of modern Greek philosophers who
think they're smart
even as they put the cart
before the horse
and of course
pretend to be kind and compassionate
even as they steal the children's chocolate
and eat it in the hiding places
obscure tiny places of shame
where no one knows their name

why so glum
dear uncle bum
didn't steal anything today
didn't disrespect anyone today
didn't poop your pants today

poopy doopy went to town
there he saw a big fat clown
floppy hats and pocket watches
lady Ann with big green swatches
you think you matter
like a debonair mad hatter
creating fancy articles of clothing

to stop the self-loathing
what's it going to take
to finally bake a beautiful cake

in a manner of speaking it was determined by the
elite group of musicians
and they all toasted the idea
with their own concoctions
being individuals who treasured their individuality
as well as their own peculiar styles
to let bygones be
and so set themselves free
from convention
from strict interpretations
from the meddlesome restrictions of the academy
to pursue new forms of music that could not be
defined by current genres

from thy box dear Bartholomew jump
and dump
your preheld notions into the bin
cause it's surely not a sin
to try new things and new combinations
clinging
springing
and then wringing
the hands in despair at the sound of nonconformity
and nothing can compare
as your notes feel so lonely and morose
almost comotose

with the composer lost in a musical world that never
existed before

creativity demands the courage to leave the nest
oh fly away oh glory
telling a brand new story
why not throw away your lipstick and
smear charcoal on your faces
leaving all those traces
of yesterday's graces
behind
but please wash your sheets every day
and have a bath every day
and brush your teeth 5 times a day

chapter ten

the headmaster ranted
and raved about the villagers who chanted
moving slowly in procession around the village
ordering blessings from their gods
please bless us oh great God
give us enough to eat
protect us from our enemies
give us joy
and peace
and love
and a deep sense of happiness

control and order
keeping things orderly
not allowing things to get disorderly

keeping dangerous and disruptive elements away
protecting oneself and the mechanisms of society
functioning smoothly and in a coordinated fashion

all cars should be white
no other colours to confuse the minds

only jeans must be worn
nice and sexy and nice and strong

all heads should be shaved for uniformity
so those with beautiful hair don't have an advantage

fashion is individuality
we must kill fashion and so
exercise and maintain control

chapter eleven

I've heard
that
Heaven
is a wonderful place
and Cuban cigars are the rage up there
smuggled there by angels
it's against the rules but since God likes cigars
there are blind eyes

chapter twelve

the old lady pointed an accusing finger at them
you left me all alone in the garden
and they came and took me away
away from my home
to live a life in exile
with barbarians who knew neither class nor love
there I worked my fingers to the bone
and suffered as an outcast
to sleep alone
I cried myself to sleep
and dreamt of deliverance
hoping one of you would come and rescue me
but no one came
then finally I escaped and found you all
and I forgive you

but please let's burn down the garden and destroy its walls
so that it is no more
lest the evil ones come back and take us all
back to the darkness
back to servitude
back to eternal damnation

the painted ceiling
as you tilt your head
still hearing all those voices
the sky is falling
the sky is falling
the sky is falling
sitting in front of the pedal organ
the smell of bacon wafting
that feeling of safeness and peace
and on the wall the picture of Oma and Opa
within the vacuum of nothingness
a spark
obscure influences conjure up images that reek of futuristic imagery
and then confounded and confused
drifting apart
wondering if there is inspiration in emptiness
a flash
plunged again into the abyss of chaos

sitting on a bench watching the sun come up
drinking slowly

the coffee
hearing the echo of a voice
please mister can you spare a dime

bobo loved his life on the run
escaping daily from reality
seeking new dimensions
creating obstacles to normalcy
as he indulged his erratic mind in mindless exercises
he was a thief
stealing food and things that he liked
and when discovered he ran like hell
bobo was a fast runner
it was his talent
thief thief
stop the thief
and he ran and as he ran he laughed
catch me if you can

which one do you want
how do you want it
when do you want it

the young boy looked longingly at the expensive guitar
then on impulse he grabbed it and ran out of the store
store employees in hot pursuit
but he was faster and disappeared around the corner
he stashed it under a tarp at a construction site

later he came with his bike and picked it up
at home he played it lovingly
he couldn't believe it was his
the next day his mother asked him where he got the guitar from
he had scuffed it all up and made it look ruined
found it
oh said mother looking at the old and abused guitar
will it even play
a little he said
I will learn
good boy she said
good boy
someone's junk is another's treasure
good for you to make it work
proud of you son
thanks mom

we dance provocatively to attract lovers
please join me
the excitement of the dance
come up for a coffee
maybe another time

a cup of coffee to go with a nice piece of cake
such a delight after a meal
would you enjoy another piece
yes please
can I top up your coffee
yes please

sugar and cream
yes please

another dream Herr Freud
what is the meaning
hidden thoughts exposed
a longing for human touch
the encircling of brilliance
and then
the light
off
on
off
on
where am I

chapter thirteen

lost in space
without a trace
of the comforts of home
not even a comb
to pull through the hair

casting a sickening cloud over Christinaity
Armaggedon
death
destruction
defeat
take those trumpets and smash them to pieces
I don't agree with it at all
I don't want it at all
I don't believe it at all
heed the call

stand tall
and don't allow mythology to make you fall
on your face
you infernal basket case

we are infatuated with nonsense
the mysteries of confusion inspire us
contradictions be damned
religions hold us in their jaded hands
demanding adherence and faithful followers
come unto me
I will set you free
and you will finally see

seeing what you want to see
as in our prisons we skip and jump
so much space to run
feeling the warmth from the sun
turn turn turn
the telly on
space X firing off another rocket
while little Jimmy sticks his finger in a socket
jumping in amazement and shock
change the lock
we were methodist but now
we're going to try to be baptist

from your bible wipe the rust
from now on in God we trust
little pilgrim grab your sack

we're marching to Zion with the wind at our back
hallelujah we're leaving the Devil's den
can I hear a big amen

still she lives alone
Eleanor are you sad
it's hard to have no one to share your life

the congregation sits there so quiet
and the parson so pious
hush everyone
the lord is here

watch the gangster sneak around
sitting in his car smoking a cigarette
thinking of stealing diamonds
a smile crosses his face
riches
you cannot be what you want to be
that's what the judge told his client
standing there in the dock
handcuffs on his hands
go to jail

smashing your dreams is what some people do
they want hell for you
vindictive religious nuts
quoting scripture as they judge and castigate you
cold and hard
it's your style that matters

chapter 14

when the road is rough
and troubles come a-calling
nobody is there when you're crying in the darkness
the loneliness is terrifying
please someone hold my hand
I promise I won't demand
a lot
just want someone to love me

I told them to put the Steinway in the barn
amongst the chickens and the pigs
it was a little dirty in there
and the piano was polished and very clean
you could see your reflection in it
so I sat down and played

and it sounded great
the chickens were running about
the pigs licked it
it seemed out of place
but really it wasn't at all
it fit in
in its own way

Yoko said go up the ladder
take the magnifying glass and identify the symbol
John did and fell in love
imagine
can we change our perspective
can we change our tune
can we change who we are

so much plastic everywhere
it's a plastic world
even our guns are made of plastic
I'm tired of my plastic dreams
they go so poorly with those fascist schemes
and my pen is running out of ink
please Isabella buy me a new pen
before all my thoughts have escaped
replaced with an absurd emptiness

I looked at the test
an F again
teacher teacher of my class
why have you been so crass

and given me an F on my test
even though I tried my best
don't you know it makes me sad
don't you know my dad will be mad
I wouldn't mind
if for once you could be kind
and set me free
by giving me
at least a C

teachers are all so cruel
they dream of hurting their students
except for their favourites which they spoil
and give great grades

I stood at the blackboard one day
daydreaming my life away
and the teacher hit me with a book
as if I was a seedy crook
I winced in pain
as the teacher hit me again
I fell to the ground and he kicked me with his shoe
kicked me till I was black and blue
and then he dragged me into the hall
telling me he'd had a ball
that hurting me made him feel so good
and please could
I never come back again
cause I drove him insane

went home and played my piano in the barn
while my cat played at my feet with a roll of yarn
at least my fingers were unbroken

chapter fifteen

they charged her with the task
of wearing the big blue mask
and as she pranced around
they found
her head got smaller
and the mask got taller
so it slipped off and fell to the ground
where it was ground
to shreds by the dancers
and the prancers
till finally it looked like Rasputin's beard
and then it disappeared

where did everything go
poof

gone
all those feelings of love
shared
and then despaired
and not repaired
even though all was bared
and we thought they cared
even as they dared
to expose their true selves and were paired
together as they shared

what was is gone forever
and it hurt when they bulldozed down my former
school
and then they took down our hospital
all those memories
trodden under
and it hurts
and then they even burnt down the farmhouse
how dare they

disrespect is clouding up my world
even as the demand for victims is rising

Freddy went to school and ate his lunch
it was peanut butter sandwiches with jam
strawberry jam
he ate it with his friends
and they all had peanut butter sandwiches with jam
except for Frank

he had big homemade bread with big chunks of ham
but he wouldn't trade with them
and they were jealous
Frank wore jeans with patches
but he had the best food
and he took violin lessons
and he played on the soccer team
and he had a paper route
and he went to private German school on Thursday nights
on Sunday's he went to church in the morning and in the evening
he played in the church orchestra
and he played in the family band
and he played in the youth community orchestra

Viet Nam was our Armageddon
it destroyed our innocence
not just America's but everyones
and John was there to be the Prophet
and then was offered up as a sacrifice
it shattered us
we were disoriented
what the hell
and then came the antichrist
the all-knowing oracle
like a wrecking ball creating carnage and despair with every uttered word
and we writhed in discomfort and mental agony
please save us Mary full of grace

when you take a speedball you see things you never saw before
tiny creatures appear in the bushes
and you get scared and run aimlessly along the street
it's all nonsensical
it's all distorted
and then you go and have a lovely bath and try to forget the trip
never again you say
never again please
who is god these days
and I wonder if the son is ever coming back
I hope not because he's destined to bring judgement and destruction
and I don't want that
and I don't want anyone to go to hell
not even Hitler or Stalin

he looked for his love in the clouds
where are you my one and only
walking alone down the street
where will they meet
at the bars he looked for her
and he did find lovers
and connections
and he had a lot of fun
so he went to a shrink
what's wrong with me
lay down on that couch and tell me everything

and so he did
and the tears fell as he talked
and the shrink said see you again
and he came again and talked and talked
see you again

chapter sixteen

war is over
please turn in your guns and tanks
park your jet fighters
bring in the nuclear submarines and aircraft carriers
all military uniforms are to be burned
and we are vacating the minister of war cabinet
position

the smell of peace filled the air
the drums were silent
the people sat and stared
what now
so I moved to New York City so I could hear people
arguing
people being rude

arguing and giving each other the finger
then I felt peaceful again

I hate silence
I love the sound of ambulances and jackhammers
the sound of work and hustle and
bustle
action
give me action
I don't want to live in an old folks home
it's depressing
who wants to retire
retirement is for people who are dead already
I want to live
shout it from the rooftop Suzie
let the whole world hear it
let it echo

overthinking is killing our minds
keep it simple
don't complicate things
don't try to be so witty all the time
why be so cool
who cares
everyone cares
please like me

life is about purpose
planning and partying and breeding and dying
God sticks his nose in the middle of it all and

threatens us with hell
dam it
and dam his minions led by the pope
who enslave millions and demand adherence to the
rules of their religion
or else
religion is about threats and bullying and male
dominance
cover your faces women
don't talk in church women
submit to your husband
know your place
and don't speak out of place
and stay away from his place
my lover please don't leave me
let your kisses smother me
for you I would die
intoxicated by your presence I am drunk with
pleasure
let us lie on beds of eiderdown and embrace our love
our love is like candy
let's help ourselves
reach out and touch me as I touch you
tingling feelings of sublime delight
I delight in you my love

dam God
dam religion
and dam the pope

chapter seventeen

down the dark back alley peddling
a splash of wine and
soaked
wash it all away and the smell
lingering with people wondering
a wino or
innocent of all the crimes
so why was he wandering in the halls of Justice
looking for a cigar

the judge pounded down on the table with his gavel
order in the courtroom
the chickens scattered after the loud boom
and the old ladies stood up in shock
what was going on

shutter the windows and lock the doors
the thieves are coming to steal
run baby run

the power and the glory
how about an atomic bomb exploding in the air
over your own city
is that the glory that you dream of
as to smitherines everything is blown
think on that
my dear cool cat
cause God promises much more
destruction
chaos
when his son comes back to rule the world
and then eternal hell for most of us
that's the power and the glory

then did bob take his bible into the desert
and did set it alight with his bic lighter
and it burnt
evil book of destruction he cursed
and as it burnt Lydia came to that place
dressed in lavender and lace
and she put down her boom box and danced provocatively
and she danced beside the fire
and she jumped over the fire
and she did a striptease there beside the fire
writhing and wiggling until she lay exhausted and

naked on the ground
and Bob saw that it was good

and Lydia did arise and bid Bob to sit beside her
and she took out a sandwich from her lunchbox and said
take and eat for this is my body
and furthermore she took out a bottle of Pinot Noir and said
take and drink for this is my blood
and thus did they together sit in the desert and eat and drink
then a cloud passed over and Lydia rose into the air waving at Bob
see you Bob
remember to remember me
and Bob being greatly astonished waved and waved
until engulfed within the cloud Lydia disappeared
then did more clouds appear and it rained and the thunder did roar
it was like nothing Bob had seen before
he felt the power even as he had also seen the glory

chapter eighteen

the barbershop stood on the corner
inside the barbers cut hair
it fell to the ground
and at the end of the day
it got swept up
bundled up
and sent to the wig maker

Ursula wears a nice blonde wig
it makes her look so striking
she's so confident
feels so sexy
walks so like a model
and the people stop and stare
some wish that she was bare

does she even care
and will she dare
to let down her beautiful hair

nothing is real
and that's okay
our imagination fills in the blanks

chapter nineteen

looking for a hiding place
I'm scared of life
they hunt me down like an animal
I'm an outcast
I hear them whispering outside my door
why do they hate me so much
why do they want to hurt me
why do they seek my destruction
all those evil tax collectors
plundering my meager resources
seeking to take even the necessities of life from me
my family suffers
and we have no recourse
they have all the power
and the judges collude with them

I am weary and broken
where can I hide from these evildoers
friendless and bereft I suffer at their hands
they are the handmaidens of Satan
I fall upon my face and weep
weak and heavy laden I suffer
and no one cares
no one offers me solace
no one wants me to live

chapter twenty

the cupboards were bare
in the fridge a package of doughnuts
that's all
and I was sad
what happened to my life
why were we here
everything I knew was left behind

the world reeks of injustice
so much thieving and lying
the powers that be are destroying us
we need to take away their power
we the people
you know
like it was supposed to be
the pain

and the misery

in outer spaces
are pictures of sad faces
snapshots of abuse and regret and sadness
a reaction to the madness
from door to door
in the biting cold they travelled
voices of cheer
without the beer
and she sitting beside him peppering him with her questions
a beauty queen
interested and attentive and hot

left hanging
from the cliff
help me
help me
fingers stretched out and quivering

faith in what
I believe if it can be proven that
and who
rolling the stone away was always the least obstacle

night shift blues
what a ruse
another sucker dedicated to working for the man
do this oh ancient master of ceremonies

say this oh ancient master of ceremonies
hear this oh ancient master of ceremonies
and then to hear those words
those special words straight from the mouth of the
prophet
and thus it is written

from the depth of despair
slowly the trend was upwards
joy replaced the sadness
confidence took the place of doubt
morning breakfasts
and the ping pong
then off to school
the sickness came back and the angel fell down from
the sky
bruised up and heavy laden with grief
into the wilderness
staggering
fifty years of haunting misery with the agents
bearing down upon him
hiding and grovelling and begging and stealing
beating death time and time again

and then a break in the sky
a touch of light
as without hope our hero fights on in the eternal
night
scared to hope for reprieve
still clinging desperately to the edge of the cliff

chapter twenty-one

reserved for so and so
what are these interlopers doing in my place
get out
no respect for proper rights
barbarians who don't understand the world
who don't understand their place in it
who flaunt rules and regulations and protocols
upsetting the established order
not willing to pay their dues

on the golf course he did not wear appropriate
clothing
ragged blue jeans were not the correct choice
sir you have to leave
why

your clothes are not in compliance with our dress
code
so what I don't care and I won't leave
the manager pulled out a gun and shot him
he told security to dispose of the body in the
dumpster
and that was that
easy peasy
no need for lots of talking or arguing
one shot to the head and everyone's happy
and all the golfers raised their clubs and cheered
hip hip hooray
hip hip hooray

chapter twenty-two

small time politics
within the city limits
the young thugs smoking their cigars
pretending to be tough
you want to mess with us baby
come on then
bring it on
you got guns
we got guns
the wall of cops moved towards the thugs
the thugs let go with their machine guns
mowing down the cops who were too shocked to fire
a single shot
that's how you do it the leader shouted

chapter twenty-three

a bag of cheezies and a bottle of Pepsi

chapter twenty-four

Reverent what should I do with my life
Give it to Jesus
Give it away

will you not abide with me
let us walk together
alone in this world I would not be

the socialists walk together down the street
whistling and fingering their heavy gold necklaces
they dream of riches
and preach poverty
what is a servant without a master

he took some acid at school

far out man
pranksters everywhere doing tricks
with them some finely dressed philosophers
who were trying to imitate their professors or
trying to tell stories
with hidden meanings like
a parable
almost like Jesus
who was also a philosopher
or a rock star without the music
or a guitar
psychedelic thoughts were influencing the youth
and some were jumping up on benches and
pontificating
because they had all the answers
everyone disoriented
where the heck is the shore
can you see the shoreline mister
and the music was surprising us
but it had expectations
so we said forget it
freedom was our thing
don't tell us what to do music
we do what we want and dam the critics

all those walls everywhere
they hem me in
like mountains
breaking out was the dream
it's everyone's dream

move the story forward
that's the way of intuition
not set in stone
no musical notes only what's in our heads
this way and that way

the old man came along and said that's not how we do it
and we shook our heads and said but this is the way we do it
and he shook his head and walked away muttering
everyone has their own way
nice if we can play together
knowing is a senseless dream
mystical illusions where outer space is in your living room
to be a gypsy
set up the tents
and all those microphones sticking up into the air
as if they're trying to find heaven
where is heaven
no one is reporting back

it's undeniable that we need to stick together
antiquity meets the future and the noise is loud
crashing all the contradictions
and then it's on the road again
pass the potatoes and let's sing for the master
I feel so confined
loosen these bonds master

that is what I need
make me your high priest
and let me offer sacrifices for your sins
you are forgiven

chapter twenty-five

being a musician is not a job
it takes control of you
you give yourself to music
24 hours a day
no time for a family
music is your family
making music is talking to spirits
a musician is always in church
what church
any kind of church
during the day you're a musician
at night you're a musician
on weekends you're a musician
never ending state of being
making rhythmic noise is music

tapping your feet is music
masterbating is music
and then she appears playing you for a fool
who could it be

the magic women come out to play
dressed all sexy
teasing us with their delightful thighs
and beautiful derrières
we fall on our knees and worship
please love us
please play with us
please let us touch you

the music plays on
and on and on forever
and ever

put on your sunglasses boys and act coy
watch the girls prance by
I'm sticking with you
let the world go to pieces
music is our women
we hide between their legs
reflect your essense on us
and allow us to become what you are inside

the pirates are crawling around in your bed
stabbing knives into your head
dead

that's you without the Pirates booty
the treasure is spilling out
somewhere
who cares
the Queen is watching the boxing match
waiting for her man
a left
then a right
watch the guy with the patch run away
jewelry in his hands
stop thief

the cops stand and stare
on this sorry night in April
close the doors and wipe up the blood

the Pirates phone is ringing
is it for you
the mayor says for you to call him
all those secrets

out in the ocean the Pirates are sailing away
I don't know to where
where are they going
where are we going
listen to the parrot singing
hi ho the dario

feeding five thousand people was no easy feat
but Christ did it

can you do it

this world is not pure
and there is no cure
for the stirring in our soul
that's why we play that rock and roll
and look under every stone
to find what we're looking for
but we don't know what we are looking for
so we keep on looking and are perplexed by the
mystery of life
we look at everything from an angle to try to solve
the problem
and that's no sin

are you committed to falsifying your pedigree
or would you rather be free
in this guilded cage we attempt to fly
to fly to fairyland to dream
of wonderful vistas and success

our God is an awesome God
the choir moves back and forth as it sings as one
the conductor waving his hands in solidarity
watch the pianist as she moves her perfect hands over
the keyboard
a machine
watch Mathilda as she opens her mouth as far as it
will go
and Morris as he closes his eyes in reverence

great and holy and mighty
set apart
a people
dedicated to build the pillars of Christianity
to work under the shadow of the cross
proselytizing
preaching the message of a crucified Christ
who purchased a pardon for all humanity
by allowing the Romans to nail him to a cross
gracious redeemer
son of God

replace your batteries in the remote
turn it on
turn it off
her long hair cascading down upon his face
his eyes closed in reverence
this sacred moment
this intense pleasure
this holy bond

return to the land of your forefathers and till the soil
producing vegetables and fruit
for your tables

she stands in front of the church clasping her purse
waiting for the pastor

let the sunshine in
may all your dreams come true

pray that sorrow stays far away

in an open field he stands with his face looking up
my god
my god
why have you forsaken me
and the rain comes
it washes his face as he wipes the raindrops away
along with his tears

the rainbow chicken kicks up her heels
dancing to the music left over in the pantry
raindrops keep falling on the balconey
but her spirit will not be dampened
somewhere
there is a land
beyond our heartaches and sadness
happy
watch the violinists play so merrily under
the baton
looking down on the street
wondering who will meet
who
under the magnifying glass
a closeup where the gazes of the critics
melt confidence
and try to break spirits
rise up
a lifetime of running comes down to the feeling
inspiration

hope
and
confidence

the fences we build
thinking they're for our own good
and the watchtowers
from whence we peer down
observing the people as they play
within the lines
obeying all those rules
keeping us in line
so we can define
who we are
where we fit in
why we exist

go on
read all those books
miles upon miles of writings
everyone an expert
we know this
and we know that
and we disagree with them
but we agree with these

the batter smashes the ball just right of left field and
rounds the bases
first
second

third
and beats the ball as he slides into home plate
safe yells the ump
the dugout erupts in chaos as the players storm out
to congratulate
the World Series is won
and there are happy faces
and there are sad faces

poopily doopily jigger jag
they caught him looking at the mag
ten lashes with the cat of nines
and ten years in the diamond mines

unleash the ghouls
everybody goes to morality schools
so we don't have so many fools
who don't want to obey the rules

I saw her standing in the rain
beside an unattractive sewer drain
she caught my eye and winked at me
as beside the goalposts I was taking a pee

oh me oh my what have we done
taken away all our fun
our freedom we threw down in the trash
as for the exits we made a dash

please protestor hold your sign high

please protestor please don't cry
against these laws we have to rail
don't walk away and bail

kachoo perplick nachaza mchazey
all the people have gone crazy
we crawl on fours looking for some hidden rock
while the police wack us with a sock

take this and this and that and that
you think you're some cool silly cat
come with us it's off to jail
where the judge will hold you without bail
tempted and judged and condemned we stand
while in the corner there plays a band
they play the blues while they sentence us to life without parole
then throw us into a ghastly darkened hole

I knew it he cried
our souls have died
the witches brew we all did drink
and toasted the discovery of the missing link

go go go
never say ho ho ho
cause they took Christmas away and sent it to outer space
and now we'll never get to second base

all those feelings of yesterday
sweep over me
sadness and joy all at once
we used to think of the world as pure
when we were so innocent
were we really that beautiful
so unruined and full of hope
we believed
even when they lied to us we believed
we danced into the night
life was such a delight
even a hangover was fun
in my ears I still hear the voice of Lou
and Cale bowing away
it helps to keep me alive
it's the perspective I dream about
and when I'm down and everything looks so
disturbing
so distorted
when life gets turned on an angle
I keep that picture in my soul

chapter twenty-six

up and up and up the sunshine
pulling me by my hair
till rising into the sewage of a new world I cringe
take me back - horrified
the heart is losing its charm
as on the bus she danced and smiled
you want some
yes please
here take a handful
of nuts - Brazil

it's music rising in a crescendo as the principle
lectures on bad behaviour
can I not have a bag of candy to go with my fried
sausage

no you can't so quit asking
but please he whined
lacy looked at him and grimaced - I hate whining
pouting he ran away down the street
and who would he meet
but Alex who was being pulled by a John Deere
tractor while sitting on a bearhide
could have been laying on a concrete floor
with a nice leather couch on top and
a pink recliner
very non-avantegarde

meanwhile she poured a bowl of sugar on the
stranger
who looking at his silhouette through the peephole
was making strange noises and
tapping his foot to imaginary music

a backwards glance and a forward approach collided
clashing as if
a revolution coming but
averted like eyes
even as if a new deal was not possible and reaching
back the conductor
fell off the podium and all the music
stopped
life is not like a knife
and those prunes will start more than a revolution
with a glass of water
pour in some soda and a shot of whiskey

credit given where interest denied
so said the troubadour as she took off her silk
panties and tied them to the tree
see
how do you want to be
free

freedom
what - and give up these late night promenades with
alverez
who though not completely incompetent is at the
very least sour as a grape
and not a little disconnected
where angels and white ducks splash
without water and without a vision
did I see it coming
did I perchance want it to appear
did I even think about it
these are the questions that haunt
even as bent and gaunt
she did flaunt
her unbecoming body dreaming
and hoping that
groping someone would
find it amusing to stumble half-baked into that
forgotten land

why will willy not decode the time machine
those anti-gravity interlockers need adjusting as does
his

tie
mending she was
bending he was
spending they were
ending the subsidies
full price now mates
and clean up after yourselves

all that crazy talk made me hungry
as Barbie strolled around naked
and Chuck gazing
fell off his chair
as his stare
put him in a state of panic
dance and sing and out of control
mystical dimensions painting themselves
sideways
that man is going to be a ruin
and should we blame the woman
mumbo jumbo in the jungle with music
Rock and roll and guitars wailing
as flailing
around - those arms and legs
everywhere
unreasonable was the attitude that brought a new
symphony
violins and cellos out of tune and the clarinets
asserting themselves
throwing music stands at the bass drum player

you're all going down she yelled
purple socks falling around her ankles
don't bring me down Jezebel
I promise to pay alimony
I promise to buy you candy
I promise to worship your royal highness
promises promises she said
get something through your head
you'll never get back into my bed
and if you come close I'll fill your ass with lead

wander in a daze
getting lost in a haze
back to Indiana to find some gold
who moved the vault
searched the world over for true love and didn't even find gold
this is pain
and everyone going insane
so creepy
growing old is a nightmare
youth was a treasure I never treasured
no no no
I won't grow old
that elusive fountain of youth is out there somewhere
look into the bible
it's in there somewhere between the blood sacrifice
and St.Pauls shorts

everyone is going to die - someday

promises made as max went wild
sniffing under doorways and

I want you to bake a chocolate cookie please
craving is driving me nuts
who should pay the price
not the guillotine again
went to Paris for a croissant and what did I see -
heads rolling on the streets
bloody mess I say
hey there mr.scientist give me five
and don't give me no jive
about all those theories
I'm perplexed
I'm confused
I'm shaking
all over and please lolletta pass the lollipop
sucking and licking
yum yum

in the day so foggy
ran a doggy
he ran on the ground so soggy
and said to his master
this ground is wet oh master
yes it is said the master
and since when can you talk
since I put on a magic sock
a magic sock

yes I bought it when I sold some stock
you had stock
do you think all I do is lick my cock
no but you're a dog
ya?

prudent and yet not remorseful
counting the pennies and yet not resourceful
flexing muscles and yet not forceful
no sense throwing your money around
then you will get yourself in a bind
and being in dire straights
you will suffer

the faith was broken so long ago and now
the restoration is impossible
the effort is there and the desire
to steal so much
to take joy in the debauchery
to prey on the powerless and lock them in a prison
the man on the moon has tears
a forgotten land where people became hollow shells
the great betrayal

and God looks down from his throne
vengeance is mine
the avenger will arrive
even though the cheese on the moon is red and not green
eyes have not seen but

the spirit is tired
the end thereof is death

listen carefully the angel said to me
take these wings and fly over to the white monks cave
sprinkle some moondust on his donkey
shout hosanna three times and then land
and stand
at the entrance
as he comes out hit him over the head with a 2 by 4
and say
our God liveth
after that a prophet will appear and cut off your foreskin
this eat and thou shalt be restored to fellowship with God

and I did as the Angel bade me and the monk lay motionless as I spoke over him
I did say the words of the Angel
I then flew away and gave the wings back to the Angel
he was waiting at McDonalds eating a Big Mac
he put his wings back on and flew away without a word
I watched him as he disappeared

chapter twenty-seven

it was the great betrayal and the children cried
it was as if someone had died
it was as if a trusted one had lied
the evil had been growing for some time
a professor lost on the slippery slopes of self-
infatuation
self-indulgent escapades of fancy taken with a bowl
of arrogance

let the pigeon fly away
the trap you set
had preconditions that could never be met
and freedom so sweet - why fret
but the price - I bet
you cannot pay

as in the lion's den the friends pace
being persuaded
and then persecuted

your toes no one had held to the fire
wrath of God descending from above
defending the right to choose
oh please let not thy countenance fall so
for unto God thy will thou shalt entrust
hitherto hath heath and heather granted
as labouring we grunt and groan
as joan let's out a moan
and jose watches the values of this progressive
civilization crumble

the fall of humpty was inevitable
the envy of the courtiers
the jealousy of the ladies
the desires of the clergy
a conspiracy that could not remain silent but raged
on and on
and then one day it happened
totally predictable
any prophet of doom could have told you so
just pour another glass of wine
white please
red makes me so hot and flushed

I tried to fake
that I liked the cake

as we sat and drank tea beside the lake

we all try most of the time to get along
it's a game of chance

those dice are so sexy
so inviting
they feel so nice
roll the dice
feel the power

she was wrong to go to the movie at that time
the tide turned
and new thoughts began to percolate
what about this
hadn't thought about it

as they tore down the old building the rats ran
Gilbert Stillgrass wondered about the neighbourhood
a new building has to find a way to fit in and stand
out
a compromise was reached as the architect felt up
Johnny's bum
she asked Johnny for a date
he ran away shaking his head and mumbling
she ran after him and called him names
finally the engineer intervened and a truce was
reached
Johnny would have coffee with her and she would pay
and after they would go to her place where she would

give him a blowjob
he sighed in resignation - women can be so bossy he
muttered

socrates had to drink the poison
he was another lamb of god
a sacrifice for mankind
we enjoy killing off the wise ones
keeps us stupid for centuries
good thing Plato made up a lot of stuff
dude knew how to lie

driving down the road I saw a pair of pants hanging
from the telephone wire
on fire
an eerie sight on a cold november morning
and on the corner a priest shivering
holding a bible up to the sky and praying
bless me father for I have sinned
his pants pulled down and nancy the whore sucking
his dick

she glanced at me and laughed
then as her client came in a burst of glory she waved
at me
beckoning
I waved back and stepped on the gas

who will water the plants at the funeral home
who will wail and cry at the funerals

who will wait for the hearse to leave
who will have the courage to speak the truth

oh ideology where did you go
and who's going to stop the flow
of your endless river of blow

a hero sang a lullaby
she sang it nice and sweet
and all the men came to listen
then she branded them with a hot iron
oh how they howled in pain
I own you now she said
my bidding you shall do

and then she cracked the whip upon their yellow backs
work you lazy bastards she shouted
and the flying nun nearby laughed

if you joined the cult of the bogus chimes
beware
something fishy is going on
hold on there's a call coming in
hello
no we don't
okay
bye

the one-eyed man had a tale to tell

five minutes of hell
the trail left some traces
and yesterday's unrest still lingers
the loners on the mountain praying to scary-man
bless us please oh scary-man
we pledge allegiance and will proselyse
and if they choose to prosecute then
we will run away - far away

sweet sweet music wafting over the trees of Mexico
a contraband of notes
summoning the archangels
consecrated we must be
and well protected from the bandits that roam on the highways of our minds
stealing our thoughts and processing special calls for purity
even as the pirates ravage the land and sell souls to the devil
who warming himself by the fire theorizes about salvation and the damned
in the end he believes victory will be his and he alone will rule
then Michael will have to obey him and Yahweh will be gone
his dream engulfs him
he smiles as he plots

the outrage engulfs the space between the witch and the crotch

watch out she screamed as the train bore down upon them
too late and bleeding they lay dying on the tracks
it could have been avoided by staying home and drinking hot chocolate
but that wasn't good enough
no excitement
now you got excitement
and a lot of blood
and dying people

the exorcism didn't go as planned
take that!
a demon demonstrating democracy
free possession to go with free speech
and of course the monster gala was sold out
even as ten thousand lepers vanished from the inner city
that infatuation
that cleanliness
that miscalculation
take it back
along a winding road where all the pants got up and walked
the melody
strange yet compelling
calling all Mariners to get into their boats
sail to foreign ports and find a woman
love in in the air and
please Sebastian do not leave

I love you and the plants need watering
my eyes have seen the glory
and if the lies were ten times greater would not my
heart still flutter
adieu and come again as tears fall upon the sheets
choirs singing
ears ringing
melancholy bringing

did religion court perversion as eroded
the values who were running
amock you say
perhaps but also disjointed and
oh I see and if the mouth was bigger perhaps
the tales enlarged and full
take a tanker and drive to the berghoff
there he still will be concocting large plans
a ghost living in the shadow of the mountain
whose grandiose ideas born
starting from a tiny idea and nurtured
until a christ appeared in the architecture and
beckoning
nearer and nearer
and the fantasy became an abstract concept that
leapt with glee out of the bus
scampered along the village street
collapsing in the market while all the peasants
trampled it

chapter twenty-eight

Shaman Bob - where is Shaman Bob
interplanetary trips through symbolic metaphoric
impersonations
in restful dreams we slumber even as our spirits glide
along natural routes at interfaces
who goes there and the watchman confused
the luggage was lost
carousel B
ticket stamped - combination excursions to lotusville
abandonment and then the shots
murder and then the flight
absolution and then the guilt
throw the dice
again and three blind mice
perchance even thrice

then pay the lady - so nice
all the customers gathered together and paid the price
gather ye on the front lawn and eat your rice

nothing to do with mindless meanderings at political conventions
slapstick comments
a lewd sideshow as the deputy showed up in her underwear
throw down a gauntlet or two
run varied with explanations copied for nothing in avenues
rotten the corpses denied entry
forgotten as frauline greta summoned without protocol
designed
denigrated
defused
the torrent tumbled down the embankment
and holding on to its sides
burst into merciful laughter
pain from above with a side of carefully constructed and prefabricated schmaltz

the obvious alignment cemented in providence
forging ties that bind
even as the blind
musicians swap instruments playing revised social dogma

existing without and hopelessly devoted to the
religious leaders
in this we trust
fallen and bruised by the chains of the status quo
students arise ashamed
perplexed
but even so - nostalgic
adventurers meandering in a maze of their own
design
lost
and all those deceased feelings gathered together on
an island
where with mother Mary a truce is declared
no more crying over spilt milk

kings of philosophers shouting from the
Brandenburg gate
heil all friends of Santa Claus
bring all your gifts to the centre for distribution
and it was as it was written
and it never backed away
and she dabbed her eyes as tears welled up
the memories

lights off
9:00

curfew

who shot the lame lady larmastool

into the pool
oh such a fool

and the Angel handed me a broom
use this to clean up the mess
when the time has come and the vengeance of God
has run its course
then you will know
and I praised the lord most high
and I promised to do his work
and I blessed his holy name

blessed is the God of all creation
blessed is the God who holds the stars in place
blessed is the God under whose sceptre we exist
for he is holy
and righteous
and lord of all

foolish is the person who turns their back on the
supernatural
who mocks the existence of deity
and lives according to their own desires and lusts
for they shall be brought down in their time
humility and worship is what God wants
for God alone is worthy and just
and his mercy is everlasting
but for a time shall ye suffer and then face to face
everyone shall fall to their knees
and return to the fold

and God in mercy shall forgive and forget
and hell will be abolished
with the kingdom of God everywhere

when the evil witch and Satan colluded it was catastrophic
with the support of their minions and their disciples
on earth they ruled
but the lamb was slain
and the sacrifice changed the course of history
good will again take over
war will be banished
greed will abate
as will hate
and Kate
will meet her fate
as she rides her carriage through a rusty gate

heed the prophecy and live
curse God and die

chapter twenty-nine

nihilism is contrary to the constitution of life
a meaningless existence will contradict and
wherefore shall the dizzying heights of folly collude
with
known existential parameters that
bend and quiver

with the arrow piercing the heart
dead shall we say or
perhaps a second opinion should be given
fiendish grins on the express
a dessert then
or
well there was a second thought
travelling at the speed of light the spacecraft

disappeared and it was thought
exploded or materially disintegrated
as a band of - what does it matter
smattering of a conversation listened to
on the radio
the t.v.
on a band of wifi surfed by a sailer from the bauhaus
- the past rising up
building new levels of uncertainty among the prestige
the latest fashion with nipples all aglow
sexual predatorship declared and
charges are pending even as the zipper flew shut
trapped
freedom curtailed
let not thy lust overwhelm thee dear clymineous
assume the worst
plan for the worst
and the worst
shall be the cup that thou must drink even on the eve
of crucifixion

November bells are ringing
the Angels they are singing
my ears they are a-ringing
with messages of love and peace
as the shepherds guard their sheep on the hills of
galilee
oh minstrels guide us in these dangerous times
where values and forget me nots clash as if
true knowledge and experience fight against foes of

reasonable expectation
weapons being wielded that can't be seen
sinister sisters of benevolence feeding violent
statutes of terror
the lawyers and judges conniving
and in the belfry still counting - the vampire
darkness coming early
knives coming out before the night
and all that delight spread upon the bread of the
dead
cleanse me
wash me
baptise me
in the blood of the lamb
and make me worthy and pure

the road to heaven paved
I hear a bid
contracts awarded
devil asphalt
demon blacktop
satan road contracting
register for the bid depository
the lowest bid will be accepted

those blocks of gold - not acceptable
too soft for a road
melt them down for jewelry

your hearts too hard

melt them down with the milk of human kindness
good deeds

saint saddam will you be my guide
your goodness has overwhelmed
for the time being let us overlook all the killing

forgive and forget
so easy

a bra ca dab bra
put it on your chest and let
fingers walk as talk
cheap

lying down
moaning with hands
on head
crying - sighing
the end is here
the end is near
the end is clear

Bang! - the building falls down
intentional destruction
something new on the horizon
planning
got to believe
even if the saints are holding an auction of used body
parts

well worn feet
long brown hair
in the village the desperadoes are still using
on the floor with a cup of flour
bake and cook
why did the teacher teach the lesson in the nude
if only a tank had arrived
in the shadow hiding
no one that I knew
a friend of the chief
or rather an enemy of the church of the redeemer
open thine eyes
and thine ears
and thy wallet
then with a closed mouth - throw the dice

the code of love estranged
believed by the exorcist as misbehaving and entombed
neon signs warning and the catastrophe appearing
with a sheet of paper signed by an unrealized propaganda officer
the lady was stunned
roses set in a vase of deep purple
and he marched in a red tuxedo
is the machine band walking off the cliff
on purpose and straight ahead thinking caps off
symbolic and who is the key architect of social demise
even the cook who is transcending cookery

contradict thyself again lord stupid as you fry those
frogs legs
salute the flag
drop your pants
conceptualize your fear

fashion poodles prancing along the avenue
did you hear the bells
ringing as round the corner
coming off a New Years gala
an assortment of evening gowns parade
giving a foretaste of the years tastes
all inspired by terror round the world and
comments by political establishment figures who
foist upon their countries their fearful predictions
and
a cacophony of selfish desires
motivated by the greed they inherited from the upper
echelon
who - nursing grudges are suppressing freedom and
progress
blame it on the food in the cafeteria
unless that improves we're all damned

hey there lady moonshine will you give me a peace
sign and
promise me that the harvest moon will bring me luck
will we always suck
or how about a kick at the can in Berlin where
the führer was redecorating

making everything big and
bold
the guns and all that leg shown
trampled was all that genuine feeling for humanity
the abstract values of mechanism taking for
granted the sun that shone at night
but the delight
in small insignificant meanderings was
snuffed
there was a price
paid it was and then sacrificed with noble intent but
allowing the piano player to eat salami
playing only black keys and
strumming a guitar also
and
let it all go
and let her lie for you
as you promise to die for her

laying on her couch and haunted
the painting - what was it
so deconstructed and wild
inspiring rebellion
walking by the sea
the waves curling over each other
smashing and churning
as turning
she asked
what does it all mean
and who knew

searching questions scorching our inner self
leaning on the status quo even as
we destroyed ourselves with drugs and bad habits

moby dick was lost at sea
miles fumbler was trying to get free
higher than a kite he
stumbled and fell after trying to be
cool and drinking tea
while walking with me
along the bea
ch

chapter thirty

the river of rice is boring and untasteful
as is the change of key
I never liked it and the natives were in agreement
sadly the priest in charge of communion was wearing
a red and white jumper
it impressed no one
not that anyone cared
or dared
to question the choice of clothing

the understanding flew out the window like a bird
the weaker he got the stronger she got and her
impulsive nature
took over
no thinking

the concern overtook and
without being independent he silently whispers
obsessive and commandeering she steers the ship
the rocks are mocking
the behaviour so shocking
the seagulls - not mocking
inland is the travesty as the sea remains aloof
poof
looking at that stern face
lips pursed
wrinkles standing at attention
an endless stream of nonsense emanating
shocking
the shackles of decency cast off
falling into crevices of demented fog
as uncivilized and uncouth - the one-sided
conversation continues

proof on paper
exceeding demand whereof the dog mutters
does it matter
of what consequence

sit there in your temple of shame
stuttering out the name
oh so and so
well - that figures does it not
and us with our pants down
again

fidelity didelty chip
the man of the manor is such a dip
he loosened his tie
and spit out a lie
fidelity didelity chip

on the moon
soon
a chinaman
squinting in the morning sun
having so much fun
and laughing at mankind
chopsticks in his hands
rice bowl at his feet
saying to the rest of us - please take a seat
and listen to the beat
as I celebrate this feat

a river of peace it floweth where flowers bloom
bullets flying overhead
with the jets of war
jagged pieces of steel cutting gently through the mist
missiles jetting across the skies

papers signed sealed and delivered
as the children quivered
naked and crying
their mothers dead
brought down by lead

justin put on his mother's pink panties and
sauntered into the street
look at me I'm the man
I know everything and you guys - nothing
flexing his muscles he scampered about pumping his fists
imaginary enemies appeared and were dispatched with
hallucinations appeared and pinched his cheeks
ouch he said
they laughed at him
pretensions arose from the ground and taunted him
he stamped upon them with his feet but they eluded him
and then the hand of god appeared in the western sky
it clenched into a fist and shook at him
he ran away wailing and howling
mommy mommy where are you
mommy was smoking a joint in the outhouse and wouldn't come out
he pleaded
he begged
he knocked
go away she whispered
go find your own way
go and be somebody
throwing himself down on the ground he raged in a fit of childish rage
I hate you mommy
I hate you so much
bad mommy

bad mommy
mommy who was higher than a kite smiled and made
a big poo
whatever she sighed

chapter thirty-one

I'm over the moon she exalted
can you believe this place
it's beyond my dreams
and it's ours

he looked at it and shook his head
really?

reality mixes with fantasy
a production quite amazing
everyone seeing what they want to see

blind sometimes
other instances - clear as a bell
and let it ring

on easter and christmas and halloween

taking no prisoners
lashing the logs together to make a raft
sailing to a deserted island
running around naked

go to the office and get the strap
no
yes
make me
you go right now - her voice rising
no - his voice rising
a showdown and how will it end
she goes and gets the principle and a few other teachers
he says - touch me and I'll sue you
they stand back in indecision
he laughs at them and walks out
where does true power lie
the courts have it all
the final word is precious

of course - he exclaimed as he sat up straight in bed
that's it
why did I not see that straight away
blinded like a bat
not wishing to see the truth
overcome with preconceived notions in line with my worldview

we'll lock him up because there is not other way
society needs to be protected
this madman
a peculiar and strange state of affairs
the impossibility of conforming for some
brilliant in many ways
rebelliousness
I will not
yes you will
no I won't
yes you will

turned on and revving up
the action coming around the corner
a breezy entrance
head high - feet kicking out
are we goosestepping here or
sending out signals so strong
could the vibe be wrong
hit the gong
vibrations and ripple effects transcending feelings
permission to land mission control
denied
what now?

it was sheer elegance
make it work they shouted
be a bauhaus

screaming through the skies - a shining artifact
history clashing with the latest craze
hold up the flower pot and seeing was believing even
if the lights were on dim
the glass needs to be replaced
the machine interpreted the interaction as hostile
hastening the degradation of the situation
battlelines drawn
and quartered with the tractor dragging the carcasses
through the bitter cold
hail mary full of grace
send your warfare to outer space
and don't forget to lace
up your army boots
cause you'll be needing that and more when the alien
shoots
and you're running for cover

love is more than a bouquet of roses
springing out of a heart so full
as angels gather and Jack Frost sings
and darkness flees just as a frightened mouse

return retune and remain
the homeland beckons
the memoirs of an old Saint
carved in the wood of the fireplace
hearken to the words of the sages
let not a young mans confidence entice you to
foolishness

those brazen acts so immature and dumb
do not mistake for truth
let not that glory move you
do not forsake the path of wisdom
and let your light shine brightest as your age grows
do not let silence overtake the old man who knows
so much more than he proclaims
as youth and beauty overshadows and lays claim
to titles and positions that they should not have
beware the idle chatter of the queens
as pompous and spoiled they gather in the shadow of the palace
and try to wage a war against common sense and honour
with lies and innuendo that only serve to enhance
their fading splendour
and in the echo of the dreams of the martyrs
the children gather and worship
and pray for Gods protection

and how the nations mock
the Nazi wearing a purple smock
a statue carved out of the rock
upon her feet a bejewelled sock

in camps the millions died
in heaven all the angels cried
so many people lied

and still they cry out from the ground

their blood on all our hands is found

why do those monsters in ourselves still live
how many more lives shall we give

waking and wondering
will jesus come back today
how long wilt thou tarry oh lord
thousands of years ago
we've invented a lot of stuff since then
stories we heard
tales bound up in books
teachers
preachers
vagabonds with lederhosen drinking beer and
sketching pictures
a wonderland opened up
alice in wonderland and jack
snowflakes drifting silently on the pansies
wonderful whimsical whispers
a haunting melody playing in the house next door
as the councillors went on a trip to Vegas
and the snow removal vehicles ran out of gas
stranded again
and eating Hawaiian pizza

Joshua is baptizing the people in the Fraser River
and
we looked for the doves from heaven
but none appeared so we were sad

we look for signs and wonders
miracles
show us proof
anything for our thirsty minds
mindless chatter amidst the guns of war and the
chanting of the savages
those heartless bankers on Wall Street
who in partnership with politicians and whores
steal our money
as destitute and broken we stagger along
please feed us
clothe us
shelter us
mister can you spare a dime?

Chapter thirty-two

violent sexual activities in the convent
the nun scraping blood off the floor
and lucifer peeking out from between pure white sheets
it all seems a little strange
while outside out on the range
the Cowboys are eating pork and beans
their farts echoing off the walls of the Vatican
where the pope is busy forgiving sins
five sins today for Edward - forgiven
thirteen sins for Charles - let's see - only 3 will be forgiven today
and Fred with 22 sins - none forgiven today

a self-appointed emissary of the great high God

well - voted in by the cardinals
well- continuing a long practise
peter peter pumpkin eater
had a letter of recommendation from Christ
feed my lambs you denier
and stay away from cocks that crow
what do we know
Ho Ho Ho
is that you flying on high Father Christmas
watch out for the soul artists - they want to
hamstring you
paint you into a corner
with the city councillors banning all fireplaces
and Ethel refusing to bake chocolate chip cookies

press on you rabid pursuer of dogma
do not rest from your endeavours
write new rules to organize mankind
build nice new shiny boxes to keep everything safe
and right
then stack them all nice and neat against the wall
to keep the non-conformists out
no rebellious revolutionaries welcome here

how can there be peace if we all disagree
how can we have order if we all think differently
how can we live together under conflicting ideologies
we must purge
and resist the urge
to surge

past the limits to challenge the status quo and form
new republics
defiant fists must be cut off
humble supplication is the new way
with bowed heads and meek spirits we ride the
autobahn
where speed limits have been removed
and we are free to exceed safe speeds and crash and
burn
even as our stomachs churn
and we learn
that speed kills

worship the Buddha in the cave
bow low to the ground and embrace
nothing we are
die to self
give up wealth and power
to the dirt we must return

pills cascading from the keyhole
red ones
blue ones
white ones
the evil pirate came out of the door and glared at the
people
he raised his cane above his head
take a pill and die
the people ran away
scared

the sketching book was not big enough
the art store is open tomorrow and hopefully they
have a bigger book
how can something so small hold all the information
it's like expecting the moon to hold all of mankind
we'd all get sick of green cheese very fast
just like the Israelites with the Mana
I would have grumbled too
God was tough
you complain - you die
why?
and is it a lie
that jesus had to die
and do you buy
that if for your sins you do not cry
then someday in hell you'll fry
instead of going to a mansion way up high
to have a piece of angel pie

hey st.paul did you throw a stone
did you hear the martyrs groan
did you hear them moan
as unknown
to you a light would be shown
to you and you alone would witness what would
become known
as the great enlightenment which would set the tone
for the next two thousand years

I got you babe is ringing in my ear
true love is still the best religion
if only it could last
wistful
longing
romanticism - tinsel on the tree
the star at the top
santa is coming too
don't forget the reindeer
we wait as under the banner we sip our tea
twas the night before christmas
every night is that night
pass the chocolate cookies please
pour out the booze and let's have some milk

mia lives in the forest
elves and faeries jumping around
witches and goblins sneaking round
with clowns spraying hairspray in their hair
checking out their faces in the mirrors that the pools
of water create
she's wearing a pure white smock
but there's something wrong with her
not herself at all
what happened and will she ever be normal again
yesterday I wish you were here
today is scary
and I am wary
as losing my sense of reality
stumbling

bumbling
rumbling
another pill perhaps

the cables going up the mountain
to the cave where the hermit lives
cheese and bread and water
a diet not considered healthy and yet
the hermit is 102 years old
writes poetry and reads the bible
his followers bring him supplies
guided by the cables

on fire the soul
a meditation quiet and remote

spirits sprinting sporadically
listening to voices
otherworldly chatter barely audible
a clandestine meeting ongoing between the gods who
plan and postulate about order and ongoing creation
evolution sparking a fierce renewal of resources
outsourced to the pilgrims
with backpacks going into the wilderness
eyes lifted up to the gods and praying
thy will be done
and then prostrate on the ground showing that
they're a bottom
hallowed be thy name and thy kingdom
may it come if

it not be here already
within or?

Chapter thirty-three

delilah preying on men in the jungle
as at the entrance to the ritz the rock star was
playing his guitar
give your head a shake
what do you make
is that bread that you bake
at the desk is the secretary
flipping through her cards and wanting
maybe a deal
or to make a nuisance of someone

siting on a fancy urn
ashes to ashes
burn up the trash
drink that bottle of sprite

special commandments for the disheartened who are fainting
while the music plays in the background

bejewelled with crustaceans hanging from rafters
opening doors that close and slam
william had good genes
genetically speaking he was in good shape
saw a picture of someone dancing
on the moon prancing
and all those young girls smacking their lips
then that son of Jack drove by singing into a mike
about getting an autograph in Texas from that
famous lip syncher
don't look
and stop fantasizing
gone to California without a fish in the pocket
serial guitar-smashing groupie
and you there in the black Cadillac get away from the door

the dark face of death
how tragic this drama
screaming - our souls - we loathe him
deliverance we cannot buy
a cruel and savage beast stalking
and mocking
and talking
to us in dreams that turn into nightmares

free spirits find homes in trees
and late
lagging behind
nothing wrong and ashamed they could be
getting along with the words carefully enunciated
in Berlin with the hackers
the apartment and the pink paint
dishevelled the hair
puffing with cigars in cases
lined up against the door and affecting
back turned
opportunities squandered with little celebrations
an apology would be acceptable and thank you
painting into the night with the guard listening
behind the door
is he there
or what
against all rules but it's something great
break the rules then
who's allowed and please play the trombone for
Sunday mass
open up the can of coke and communion is on its
way
a shrimp or two will finish it all nicely
singing harmony in the parking lot
grab a bag of chips

crouched behind a concrete barrier in la la land
sandwich in hand
basking in the heat

watching the L.A.women dancing naked on the
dumpster
everyone so alone

overseas at the naked restaurant they're raising their
glasses in a toast
to the man with the most
stand up young Fred and show us
the crowd is appreciative
another round

a slap on the ass
a grind against the thigh
a grope of the breast
verboten Lieberman Hans
she smiled through the fog
her crooked teeth
a tear in her stockings
stalking the neighbourhood like a storm trooper

doctor doctor there are bad people on the doorstep
don't let them in

the glass is clouded so no one can see in
it's a private party
and auntie smarty
she's prancing about in the cloak room
while in the lobby uncle david is uncorking the
bottles
as the guests take off their clothes

finally the guest of honour - the local priest
he gives a benediction to get the party started
the hostess washes his cock with a washcloth
nice and clean
everyone comes and gives it a lick
nice dick they murmur
he blesses them
this is the new communion
please pass the wine
and let us dine
on caviar and braised swine

did everyone get the memo advising us of a water
shortage
ahem - not bessi
a new dose of anti-depression pills and
no relief
the negativity continues amidst the loud laughter
loud music - a dampening of respectability
round and round the gossip goes
where friends and foes
gather together to watch as frankie throws
a fit

the wail of the siren
in his ear
gasping for breath
turning his head to look
the sky
where oh where

God
somewhere a violin singing sarcastically
a lonesome bundle of notes
falling off
away in the distance the saints are singing along
an I.V.
quickly
we can save him
come on
he's gone
oh no-no-no

tap the brill
light up
drag
again

like giant balloons on a dimly lit street
slithering
the invisible beat
inflated senses
the spiritual appetite craving
where oh where can the ghosts of innocence be
hiding
perhaps underneath this pool of pee

hopelessness is the final frontier and beyond
new dimensions of jeapardy
sign your name on the ticket to nowhere
nothing is in store

empty cupboards and windswept plains
insanity has no borders
a dispensation
of no anticipation
waiting is not an option

please pass
the empty glass

greta staggered into the room and muttered a slogan
the ongoing noise of the party drowning out her
whispering
unconscious significance
when toast and marmalade clashed
theoretical maxims mixing with nostalgia
some old prostitutes holding up worn bibles
heed ye the word of the lord and
repent of your sins
for lo the lord cometh
even in clouds of glory

in the old church the pews gathered dust
the hymn books still sitting in their holders
stained glass windows broken
the front door missing
wind whistling in carrying
leaves
in the back the choir robes still hanging from their
hooks
faded and decaying

someone's purse lying on the floor
a deserted shrine
a tribute to God
a forsaken relic

I found a discerning fascist hiding
near a forest
behind a wall made of concrete
clutching a doll made of titanium and
did you hear some chanting
a futuristic band playing in a fountain
saying things that no one else dared
and a little man in lederhosen with his ear to his phone
what?

dancing with the clowns in the trees
while glittering flakes of gold
fall
all about
and what about the circus tent
all those horses
those beautiful girls
were they our teachers

don't cry
or sigh
watch as the artists fly
on high
they believe as they hide

in bushes
under rocks
or beside the amphitheatre in ponoka

beside the river the old man was lighting up
blowing smoke to the faces of past dreams
poof
up up and away
as the eternal question was posed
and hope was still a promise

coming up the road in a full gallop
wild horses
coming to set us free
no more holes in the universe
or howls of laughter
the houses of love kaput
undone - shackles of despair
still looking for those mansions of fear
torn apart
the heart
amidst the glittering shambles of poverty
and the Stars pranking the restless masses

why don't you take this and a little of
that
and be a cool cat
just for one minute
while Edwardo shaves off his mustache

and Elenore fakes an orgasm

pour some schnapps into the glass
bottoms up my friend
can't we be friends if only just for one day
then together we will throw rocks at the houses of love
crack goes the window
oops
and look at that door - broken down

the smelters fire is vanquished by the widows tears
as the structure burns
and she runs away naked and in heels into the forest
such a typical story
a real cliché

www.ingramcontent.com/pod-product-compliance
Lightning Source LLC
Chambersburg PA
CBHW032357040426
42451CB00006B/37